Daily Reflections ... ...meditation, contemplation and personal application.

These were written to inspire and guide one along their spiritual path. A spiritual path consists of three paths: The inward path of growth, awakening and discovery; the path of life, our relationship with our world and the Divine; and the path of the ever changing relationship between these first two.

Consider committing to a year of reading one each day, one or many at a time. Use this tool as you choose, as best fits you. The suggested time to do these is during your morning practice of daily meditation and prayer then carry the idea with you throughout your day.

*Russell Kyle*

Published by Awake Publishing
2015 USA

## _Day 1_

**Acknowledge God in each moment thus making each moment a building block for a Divinely constructed day. The results can be miraculous.**

Many times in each second, miracles are unfolding around us. The Living Divine is at work always in the moment. By practicing placing and keeping our attention here in the NOW we catch glimpses of these miracles at work. Practice this all day and begin to see the glimpses come together in an understanding of the truth that your God constantly is working for your highest good.

## _Day 2_

**The best things in life aren't things. Value and enjoy yours today.**

The pleasure of things is secondary to the joys of spiritual living. In fact you will find that keeping your value in the non-material in turn brings about satisfaction in the things you already have. Things are OK to have. Just watch your attachment to them, for in a world of change, detachment is always somewhere down the road. Don't get stuck on stuff, Cherish and Give thanks for your true treasures.

## _Day 3_

**The human condition is lost in the dream of thought.**
**We are sleeping. Awaken!**

At times that you feel governed by compulsive thinking, thoughts of worry, anger and fear, you must simply get out of your head. Choose to let these thoughts go. You may revisit them later if you choose, but for now you will make a change. How? You can do this by coming into the moment. Don't attempt to think a negative thought out of your head because then you are still thinking about the thought. Leave the future and past where they are, simply turn your attention to the present moment. Acknowledge God here with you in the present and practice staying mentally right here in the NOW. In doing this the negative thoughts will slip away and you will awaken to the only true presence, with you always, which is God.

## _Day 4_

**Pay attention to good today, and good will pay attention to you.**

What we place our attention on is drawn into our lives, Good or bad. Choose well and if chosen in error, simply choose once again. Keep watch on your attention, it brings life to that which it is placed upon.

## _Day 5_

**Don't complain about a problem; choose instead to be a part of the solution.**

I am either spreading positive or negative in each action and attitude I choose. I am either part of the problem or part of the solution. As part of the solution the problem ceases to exist and all I'm left with is Good. If you perceive a problem the only resolution is your change in perception. Simply perceive yourself as part of the solution, and act on this perspective, and you suddenly realize the problem never really was as you once thought, and all is well.

## *Day 6*

**Illuminate your day by fueling the Light in others. Lift up those around you and share in their Joy as it becomes your Joy too.**

Contribute to bringing forth a positive perspective in all you associate with. In doing so it not only reminds you where your Joy is, it raises the awareness of Good in yourself and in those you're helping. The awareness of Good, or God, illuminates the seemingly darkest of days into the brightest and awakens the highest of Good possibilities for all involved.

## *Day 7*

**Let Truth, Peace, Joy and Prosperity, be your natural states of being.**

Peace, Joy and Prosperity are your birthrights, your natural inheritance as a child of God. Drop all limiting thoughts and doubts. Acknowledge this truth and awaken.

## _Day 8_

**Be flexible and flowing like water.**

Water patiently, quietly, and gently works its way through any obstacle and so can we. Change is not difficult, only resistance to change. Spiritual growth, awakening, requires that we continually let go of the old, giving room for the new. Remain teachable, movable, flowing. The sturdy tree breaks in the storm, yet the flexible tree bends unharmed until the storm passes. Bend. Make plans but be willing to change them. Drop pride and stubbornness and simply be. Change, allow, and enjoy this freedom.

## Day 9

**Surrender this day. Surrender is not to do nothing. It is to accept the present moment as is, to stop resisting what is. Only first after surrender is it possible to move ahead.**

When struggling with an unwanted situation, simply surrender by saying to yourself "It is what it is." Then move on and do what is next to be done, leaving your denial of that moment behind.

## Day 10

**Do not take someone's need to judge you personally. Their need has nothing to do with you except that of an opportunity for you to help.**

Judging, name calling, and labeling only defines the one doing the judging, name calling, and labeling. Lift up those who put you down and their judgments are redefined by you.

## *Day 11*

**Our outside world is but a reflection of our inner world. We see through the lenses of our judgments, labels, and understanding. Learn to let go of these obstacles and see truth full and alive.**

Keep an open mind. There is always more than one way of seeing things. Accept and consider other peoples' points of view, even if at first you don't understand them. Don't be crippled by your own points of view. Remain teachable.

The only difference between the value of a weed and the value of a flower, is a judgment.

Take care on your judgments, for with them, you make your world.... It's not the world you're given, it's the world you see

## *Day 12*

**Allow God to breathe through your feelings, thoughts and actions.**

Surrender yourself to your God, moment to moment.

Practice God awareness throughout the day. Also,

develop a routine of meditation. By meditation we tune ourselves into God. In practice you can carry this state of mind into all you do. The results are literally miraculous.

## _Day 13_

**Great things are unfolding for you this very moment.
Trust the process.**

Are you a see it and I'll believe it kind of person?
Instead try believing it to see it. We take the first step and
God will take the rest.


## _Day 14_

**God's voice is silent and still, the most beautiful and
moving.**

Continue your practice of daily meditation. Take
this time to be still, silent and listen. Meditate with a true
expectation to receive and you will be amazed.

By daily meditation we tune ourselves to the voice of
Divine direction, intuition, our sixth sense.

Take time throughout your day to be silent and
still your mind for a moment or two. With practice your
day can be refreshed each time you do this.

## _Day 15_

**Practice seeing the light in others.**

Turn your attention to the Good in others and Good will be your experience. We all have a pure spark of Good within. Sometimes someone else's acknowledgement of this releases its glow. Acknowledge the Good Light in others.

## _Day 16_

**There is a time for everything, if you're forcing something, stop and wait for the flow.**

Yes action is necessary for change. But be careful that you are not forcing something. Most often when things are meant to be, if it is the right time, then the change will happen. Otherwise we only stress ourselves, and others, in the attempt. In all of nature, from childbirth to the coming of spring, it can only happen when it is time to happen. Keep watch for this and be willing to change your direction.

## _Day 17_

**Want to see clearly? Close your eyes and open your heart.**

When in question, simply ask the part of you that knows. Pray about it, put it out of mind for a while, and then return to the question in meditation. With practice, and an honest interpretation of the answer, you will receive the answer directing you in the interest of your highest Good, and the highest Good of all involved.


## _Day 18_

**Seek by inspiration rather than by information.**

Your clearest connection to truth and true perception is from within. Information is handed to you, it originated from somewhere else. Inspiration originates from you, it is yours. This book was information I've presented to you, it becomes inspiration once you put it into action. The experiences don't leap off the pages, instead they rise up from within you, and they are yours.

## _Day 19_

**Humility is the most fertile ground and open door for spiritual growth.**

To be humble is to be teachable. It is to be open minded. To know that there is much to learn, and that everyone is our teacher.

## _Day 20_

**Humility**

Humility opens doors. Pride closes doors.

Today, practice humility. Be humble, gentle, and kind.

## _Day 21_

**Humility is to see all as interconnected and equally growing.**

Pay attention to nature, to people, to the flow of life. Pay attention to the coincidences, the chance encounters, the miracles.

Everyone is at the place they are in their growth that is just right for them, accept this. None are better than others; they are simply just where they are to be.

We all are connected in many ways, inside and out. See others in yourself and yourself in others.

## _Day 22_

**Consider this: When we critically judge someone we are revealing an unhealed part of ourselves.**

...Pay attention & take note.

## _Day 23_

**Lay aside judgment of the moment, suspend resistance to what is.**

In labeling, judging, or naming our present situation we only limit the possibilities. God, moment to moment, works for your highest good, simply allow God, trust God, and enjoy the freedom and magnificence.

## _Day 24_

**Listen, the Divine speaks from everywhere and everything; the wind in the trees, the flowing stream, the rain falling. A bird's song. The stillness.**

Listen and see.

## *Day 25*

**Meditation enables us to hear the whispers of the mighty Divine. This clarity sees beyond logic.**

Set the mind aside and open the heart. Meditation opens your true eyes and ears.

## _Day 26_

**A happy heart should give thanks, but an unhappy heart should give thanks many times more. Live gratefully and thankfully.**

Gratitude is the Greatest Attitude. We always have everything we need for happiness, whether we are aware of it or not. We become aware of this fact by the process of gratitude. Appreciation breeds happiness and happiness breeds appreciation.

## _Day 27_

**To grow spiritually is to simply return to what we are and always have been. It is not a journey of learning, but of unlearning. Awakening to what Is.**

The spiritual journey is the journey home. Don't think you can't get there, you already know the way, and you've already been. So relax, smile, and move on.

## _Day 28_

**There is a supply for every need.**

The universe abhors a vacuum. Every space,
every demand, is being filled the moment it has emptied.
Feel like something is missing? Need something? It's
already on the way. Maybe not in the form you think, or
in the way you would expect, but it is on the way, the
perfect way for you.

## _Day 29_

**Stand not firm to your beliefs and points of view.
Remain teachable. Resist not the flow of life.**

Holding firm (Pride) is like the mighty oak that
breaks at high winds. Be instead the flexible palm as it
gives way and bends (Humility and open-mindedness), its
strength is in its ability to surrender to the storm. It
always bounces back and in the end stands even stronger.

## <u>*Day 30*</u>

**You are not punished for your pride but by your pride. EGO is the impostor who is pretending to be you, don't feed into it. Practice humility and awaken to the real You.**

All things the ego promises are the very things it takes always. All things the ego tells you to fear are the only things that remove fear. All things humility promises you've always had and humility is the only process by which you can come to know it. Humility shows you the value in what the ego labels valueless. Humility raises the awareness that fear need not exist because that which is of true value can never be taken from you and supports and sustains you completely, wholly and lovingly. That reality, your constant companion, is God.

## _Day 31_

**Give to receive. Give to give and receive in great measure.**

In order to grow spiritually, to experience new understandings, to have higher awareness, and prosper in all forms we must keep good flowing in our lives. We draw in by humility, meditation, prayer, open-mindedness, and the practice of God presence awareness. And we extend out by giving in all good forms. In this way we keep abundance in all forms circulating in our lives. Practice giving first as a practice and it will soon enough become a desire.

## _Day 32_

**Pray**

Remember, prayer is always a good option. Don't forget to use it.

## *Day 33*

**Rest your heart and mind, simply surrender.**

Choose to Trust and rely upon something larger, wiser, simpler, and more powerful than yourself. There was something that managed the development of your being the first nine months of your life to perfection and in perfect timing, trust that same something today for the same management and development of your life.

## *Day 34*

**Relax and take it easy. Trust the process of Goodness and you will enjoy the outcome.**

Pray today? Turned your day over to God?
Well then your part is done, enjoy.

## *Day 35*

**Practice non-resistance. Cease any temptation to fight or the need to win, yield to overcome. Win by means of surrender and know full freedom.**

Let and allow. Say YES to life.

## *Day 36*

**As a creation of the perfectly Divine you have all you need for complete happiness and satisfaction.**

There is an ever present, an ever silent, peaceful place deep within your heart that no fear or circumstance can shake. Learn to come from this place. Acknowledge this place as your true mind and heart knowing that here your treasure is and here your rest.

## _Day 37_

**Rest in a state of inner non-resistance to the flow of life, a willingness to take the necessary outward actions, and an inner detachment from the outcome.**

Do what you know you must and all else will fall into place. Do your best, for today, and you're a full success.

## _Day 38_

**Let go of all but the present moment opening the way for all possibilities.**

Surrender is not settling for less. On the contrary, it is the choice to finally live again. Internally letting go of resistance to what is, accepting, and finally arriving into the present moment, life begins again and continues anew. Only here in the now do I live, move, and have my being. So only here in the present moment am I able to allow the full flow of goodness to work in my life.

## _Day 39_

**Surrender not just the attempt to control, but more importantly the NEED to control.**

Control is not a need, it's a lie. Be free instead.

## _Day 40_

**Plant the Good seed in others then leave it to the Divine for its growth.**

Don't concern yourself with others understanding or accepting who you are or what you have to say. Be good, express good, and then watch the ripple of Goodness in action.

## _Day 41_

**Every action we take, Good or bad, throughout the day expands, in a ripple, affecting all those around us.**

Our actions stretch further than the eye can see. Be mindful in action and word, and choose well. Choose Good.

## _Day 42_

**In times of trouble, inside or outside of yourself,
simply learn from it and
Choose to move on then turn your attention to
something Good.**

No experience goes to waste when bad is turned
into a lesson and Good into acts of Love.

Learn and acknowledge the lessons and move on.

## _Day 43_

**Be aware that each moment is sacred and alive.**

All things happen and have their being in the
moment. All movement and living energy happens only
in the NOW. God lives, moves and has being only in the
present moment. Have your attention here in the NOW
and see glimpses of the hand of the Divine working for
your highest Good.

## _Day 44_

**Place your attention on good knowing that what you think about you draw into your life.**

Things are drawn toward us as the light of our consciousness shines on them. What we place our attention on becomes centered in the spotlight, it becomes more a part of us, and then the universe moves to make it so. It's a spiritual law, as predictable as the physical law of gravity, always bringing what has gone up back down, so does the object of our attention become a more real, more functioning and primary part of our experience. So take care on what you place your attention for it will be so, and so much more.

## _Day 45_

**Be humble and harmonized.**

See yourself in others and others in yourself. Seek differences and you will find them, and separate yourself, and come under the pains of the ego. Seek the similarities and you will find many, you will be harmonized and unified, and in the presence of your God.

## *Day 46*

**Just as the spirit is the life of the body, giving and compassion are the life of the spirit.**

Giving and compassion, the outward acts of humility, keep clear the life line to the heart of your being. Study them, meditate upon them, and practice them.

## _Day 47_

**To the extent that you believe, you receive. Extinguish worry by surrender.**

**Banish doubt by Trust in your God.**

**God has the map, let God lead the way and enjoy the journey!**

The question isn't can God help you, the question is will you let Him/Her. Practice letting go of the attempt to control or manage situations by an attempt to eliminate fear. Do what you can but leave much up to God. God has the higher perspective. Trust your God, really let go and trust. In this way can true demonstration manifest and true faith in you be born. Don't demand to "see it to believe it," instead "believe it until you see it," and then you'll come to "KNOW it."

## _Day 48_

**Giving up the victim role is realizing that the paint brush that has been painting your nightmare is in your hand, but at the same time you suddenly realize that, thank God, the brush is in my hand so now I can paint what I want.**

It's always been in your hands, now give it to your God, and rest.

## _Day 49_

**Admitting a mistake is a freeing experience, second only to forgiving the mistake of another. Extend Goodness to your world today.**

Fear, lies, and holding a grudge only keep us caged. Honesty with ourselves and others is our only chance for freedom. We teach others how to treat us by how we treat them. We are forgiven by first forgiving. Forgiveness frees the forgiver first. Be first in yourself what you would like to see in others.

### *Day 50*

**Be Present**

Today, practice keeping your thoughts on this day. Think about tomorrow only to plan. Think about yesterday only for some purpose in today. Stay present.

### *Day 51*

**Dependence on God brings Independence from all else. Declare yours today and enjoy the Freedom.**

### *Day 52*

**Make plans but be willing to change them.**

Stay flexible and flowing.

### *Day 53*

**I hear and I forget, but if I see I remember, and better yet when I Do, I understand.**

Practice and know.

## _Day 54_

**Service to man is for us The Great Experience. It's the experience of God in Action, God-The Great Giver.**

## _Day 55_

**Trade your limitations for inspirations.**

Leave your day to Divine Power and all things are possible.

## _Day 56_

**To the extent that we let go of doubt do we allow miracles to come about.**

## _Day 57_

**In God's presence there is fullness of Joy, and God is always present.**

Practice God awareness.

## Day 58

**Surrender being right or having it your way and just be happy. Whatever it is, let God have it and Trust the Divine plan.**

The need to be right only wrongs us. Let it go and have peace.

## Day 59

**Turn your attention from within to help those without.**

Inspire Hope.

Extend Goodness. Enjoy the journey!

## Day 60

**The way from lack to abundance is a three part path. That path is one of Action, Faith, and Appreciation.**

Take the action, Surrender the outcome, express your gratitude.

## _Day 61_

**Holding blame is only protecting your own pain.**

**Surrender, let it go.**

Forgiving others frees us most. Practice letting go.

## _Day 62_

**Will-Power raises stress, God-Power brings rest.**

If it's Good, it's God.

## _Day 63_

**Don't shy away from true spiritual growth and awakening. It's packed with excitement that burns out boredom.**

Your spiritual journey is always on purpose and perfect just the way it is. You are right where you are supposed to be.

## *Day 64*

**Keep a mind full of Gratitude for a body full of Light.**

Where the mind goes the body follows. Keep your mind in the right direction. Keep your attention on Good.

## *Day 65*

**Simply Pray, Trust, and Give Thanks.**

Simply Pray, Simply trust, and simply give thanks. Perfect faith. How do we have it? We already have it. We simply must exercise it and it strengthens; water it and it blooms. The more we smell the fragrance of this flower, the more we see the delight of its beauty, the easier it is to simply rely on it for our daily foundation of peace of mind, physical health, and emotional balance and joy. Is this possible? Well give it a shot and see. I'm convinced in this process, not because I was told it works, but because it has in my life and in the lives of so many.

## *Day 66*

**We believe in God by knowledge. We Know God by experience.**

Experience God, you can find Him/Her in the Present.

## _Day 67_

**Remember, your "inbox" will always have something in it.**

Our Joy is only truly found in the process of the journey, never in the destination.

Don't get caught in trap of thinking you must get everything done and only then may you relax. Instead, if you have stuff to do, practice enjoying doing it. Don't put the pressure on yourself of accomplishing your goal, be willing to change your goal along the way. Remember the only true fulfilling goal is one of peace. In minimizing our goals, if need be, or breaking them down into many smaller goals, we have a better chance of attaining and keeping our ultimate goal of peace and satisfaction.

In the race to be better or best, do not miss the true Joy of just being.

## Day 68

**When we are in a bad mood we can always find reason to justify it. But why defend a bad mood?**

Drop the excuses, settle into the moment, count some blessings, and allow your mood to change.

## Day 69

**Remain teachable, flexible, and open to change**.

By this your day flows and each moment becomes a new and fresh beginning.

## Day 70

**It is what it is. Accept it, and move on.**

When accepting what we may label as "bad" along with the Good, knowing it's simply part of the same system, we soon find that the "bad" doesn't seem so bad after all. Remember our pain is most often not due to the situation, but due to our resistance or denial of the situation.

## _Day 71_

**Great things unfold for you.**

The down days get better; the better days have
only just begun.

Today is a Good day.

## _Day 72_

**Relax and enjoy the present.**

Your God is handling the rest.

## _Day 73_

**To awaken to Good living is only second in
satisfaction to that of playing a part in the awakening
of another.**

## _Day 74_

**Don't believe everything you think.**

When you catch yourself thinking something contrary to your original God created nature, which is Positive, quickly tell the thought "Thanks for sharing, but no thanks"…and then let it go.

## _Day 75_

**Your purpose in Living is to Awaken.**

Everything is working for this purpose.

## _Day 76_

**Life is like a coin. For balance and form it must have two sides, without each of these sides it would not be. One side some call bad, and the other good.**

Though you may only see one side at a time, they both are there. Comfort and satisfaction are not found by staying on the preferred side, they come while accepting both, as they come and as they go with each playing their part for balance of the whole.

## *Day 77*

**Cherish life, focus on what matters and let go of what does not.**

Each and every moment we have a choice between either conflict or peace. Let go and Choose Peace.


## *Day 78*

**Peace is your natural state of being. It doesn't have to be found, only uncovered.**

Relax and allow it.


## *Day 79*

**Being right, defending your frustrations, criticizing the way something is being done, is any of this worth giving up your peace over?**

Choose Peace. Let these go.

## _Day 80_

**Confidence doesn't come from always being right, but from being OK with being wrong.**

There is a freedom in open-mindedness. Welcome new points of view and be open to being wrong sometimes. It's OK.


## _Day 81_

**By demanding how things ought to be, we are blinded to how things already are.**

Once accepting things as they are, "ought to be" imprisons us no more and we see.


## _Day 82_

**Worrying is putting faith in fear. Hopefulness is putting faith in Good, or God.**

Put the power of your faith in something that works for you, not against you.

## _Day 83_

**When feeling upset that something isn't going the way you want, simply shift your focus from "What's in it for me?" to "How may I serve?"**

Enjoy the peace.


## _Day 84_

**Positive Thinking: The positive use of thought. Use your thoughts, rather than your thoughts using you.**

Keep your attention on seeking and acknowledging the Good.


## _Day 85_

**No matter what, if you're trusting your God and staying present, you're right where you're supposed to be. Physically, mentally, emotionally, and spiritually.**

## _Day 86_

**Consciously acknowledge and cherish the simple pleasures, the simple gifts, from moment to moment, throughout your day.**

Enjoy a life of deep gratitude.

## _Day 87_

**Forgivingness**

Forgiveness frees the forgiver before it frees the forgiven. Be free.

## _Day 88_

**As gratitude grows, fears slip away, and abundance unfolds.**

Grow your gratitude; cherish what you have, and appreciate each small gift as it's given.

## _Day 89_

**You are a masterpiece at work.**

Rest easy, for God always finishes what God has begun.


## _Day 90_

**Worry: Using your imagination to create something you don't want.**

So why do we do it? It's a bad habit, and habits can be changed, with practice. Think Positive.


## _Day 91_

**Stay centered; surrender your fears to faith, your thoughts to the present, and your attention to appreciation.**

Relax, settle into the moment, and give thanks.

## _Day 92_

**Pay attention to Good and you'll soon see that there's a lot more of it.**

## _Day 93_

**Worrying does not take away tomorrow's troubles. It takes away today's peace.**

Stay Present

## _Day 94_

**Today, find someone and give them your extra attention, show them that they really matter.**

You'll both walk away feeling good. Enjoy this challenge.

## *Day 95*

**Getting our way isn't the true way to happiness.**

Real happiness comes by appreciating what we have in this moment and accepting life as it unfolds in the next.

## *Day 96*

**Trade your limitations for inspirations**.

Rather than discussing what's wrong, or what could go wrong, look for and discuss what's right, and what could go right.

## *Day 97*

**Complaining is an outward expression of a simple lack of faith**.

Affirm what is going right instead.

## *Day 98*

**Practice seeing God in all.**

Practice this today.

## _Day 99_

**Keep a spark in your spiritual life.**

Keep a spark in your spiritual life by continually renewing your ideas and beliefs on God, life and the laws of Good. Continually explore new points of view, careful not to get too attached to just one. Many will grab your attention at just the moment they should, as a stepping stone for your continued awakening, but take it in and then let it go. Take care to learn and experience what you can, and then move on. In my experience I return to some of these old understandings and ideas, from time to time, from a new point of view, and see more, but in order to have this happen I had to first move on.

Read new books, go to different spiritual retreats, conventions or rituals, talk to many people, inquire with an open mind, try new meditations, new forms of connecting with Good, new ways to give and help others, explore religions, spiritual beliefs, but all with an open mind.

As our understanding of God's universe expands, so does our awareness, and as we then surrender again all that understanding, we find we are left with pure open awareness, as many times as we do this does our awakening unfold even more, broader, simpler, and full of peace. All of creation extends teachings of understanding, all we must learn to do is pay attention, and listen. Enjoy.

## _Day 100_

**People take things as they are, not necessarily as it is given.**

People react according to their expectations and current attitudes.

Don't take things personally, they're not.

## _Day 101_

**Commit this day to lifting others up**.

Speak words of encouragement, compliment them, point out their positive qualities, make them smile.

Lift and be Lifted.

## _Day 102_

**The joy is in the joy.**

As you move about today, be present and take it slow, so as not to miss the countless subtle gifts popping up along the way.

## _Day 103_

**Exercise your gratitude.**

Today, each time you find yourself looking at the clock, use it as a reminder to pause and acknowledge a blessing in that moment.

Exercise your Gratitude, and it'll grow

## _Day 104_

**What you see is what you get.**

Our attitudes, focus, and attention are the windows through which we see our world.

Choose a nice view.

## _Day 105_

**Every day is a life changing event.**

See today's events as contributing to your growth and increasing wellness.

Trust the processes, acknowledge their value.

## _Day 106_

**The highest and most revered of most all spiritual communities are its humble servants.**

Service: Giving of yourself with no expectations of recognition or return.

## _Day 107_

**Relax, Let go, and Trust.**

We of ourselves can only do so much, but Surrender and Trust in Goodness, and all the forces of the Universe will conspire and stand to support you.

## _Day 108_

**Acceptance**

Continually attempt to arrange life to suit ourselves or accept life on Life's terms. In a world of constant change, what will support a life of peace? Take care, and choose well.

## _Day 109_

**Wants vs. Needs**

Take care not to get confused between your
"wants" and your "needs."

And never forget your "already haves!"


## _Day 110_

**There is friction between our plans and Life's plan for
us. Resistance hurts**.

Be sure that Letting Go and Changing Direction is
always on your list of options.


## _Day 111_

**Rushing around takes more of our time, slowing down
gives us more.**

Racing through life leads to the end. Why race
from now to the end? Enjoy and savor the in between.

## _Day 112_

**Three ideas to carry with you today.**

Three things to keep in mind:

1. You shouldn't believe everything you think.

2. You're usually doing much better than you think you are.

3. Feelings aren't always facts.

## _Day 113_

**The fallacy of worry.**

We worry about tomorrow, yet only with the knowledge and understanding of today.

No worries. You'll likely have what you need once you're there.

## _Day 114_

### Enough is enough.

There are two ways to get enough.

One is to accumulate more. The other is to desire less.

Enough isn't a goal one reaches; it's a God-given Wholeness one realizes.


## _Day 115_

### You win!

The fact that you woke up this morning, breathing and alive, is proof that this day has already been predetermined in your favor.

Remember this today, and expect Good things.


## _Day 116_

### Remember…

Whatever it is, "This too shall pass" once it has taught you what you need to know.

## _Day 117_

**Starve the negative.**

Take care not to feed your worries and
complaints.

Count your hopes and blessings instead.

This will serve you well.


## _Day 118_

**There are benefits to being wrong too.**

Humility, with an open willingness to learn and
be corrected, privately or publicly, is a recipe for
fulfillment and wisdom.


## _Day 119_

**Your thoughts and your attitude now are your
preview of the days coming events**.

So take care and choose them well.

## _Day 120_

### Teachers

Everyone is our teacher, teaching us either what
to do or what not to do.

## _Day 121_

### Keep Watch.

Pay attention, stay present and keep watch, for the
Divine speaks through people and situations and the
Divine always has something to say.

## _Day 122_

**Stay Present.**

Overwhelmed? Life can seem too overwhelming at times, yet, this serves a good purpose too.

When we are looking at too much of life at the same time, past and future, the mind will do what it was designed to do, it will overwhelm, forcing us out of our heads, and back into present. When present moment living gets too low on the priorities list, life steps in to readjust and we come again to know the necessity of being present.

## _Day 123_

**Don't complain.**

Complaining only adds to a problem. The more you acknowledge it, the more it'll affect you. Use your attention wisely; turn it to something Positive instead.

## _Day 124_

**Accept to be accepted.**

To be accepted unconditionally, accept
unconditionally.

## _Day 125_

**Compliment instead.**

If tempted to criticize, compliment instead.

## _Day 126_

**Acknowledge the gifts.**

Every sunrise, every heartbeat, every breath, all
are a gift. Remember this and live accordingly.

## _Day 127_

**Measure success.**

How is success measured? Success isn't a measurement; it's a movement and a direction.

It's not about where you're at; it's about your moving in the right direction.

## _Day 128_

**Real letting go is beyond excuses.**

Often misunderstood, letting go and surrender are internal processes, not to be mistaken with settling for less or giving up, and by no means governed by circumstance.

We do what we can, the best we can, all we can, but with an inner detachment from the outcome. This inner detachment is letting go, surrendering.

Inner detachment; simple, but not always easy, yet always possible and always within our reach.

## _Day 129_

**Consider this…**

What can you bring to this day?
The only thing lacking in any given situation is
that which we are not giving.

## _Day 130_

**It's not what we don't have that brings feelings of
lack; it's what we don't see.**

Close your eyes, open your heart, and see. Count
your blessings. Give thanks.

## _Day 131_

**In Giving, there is only gain.**

The best gift one can give oneself is to give of
oneself.

## _Day 132_

**Be careful what you tell yourself, you'll probably believe it.**

What would you tell someone to encourage them, to lift them? Now, tell these things to yourself.

## *Day 133*

**For parents and life's students.**

I think all parents want to do their best to give their children all the good experiences that life has to offer. But more importantly, I believe, to best insure that our children have a satisfying and happy life, is to teach them to Appreciate and Value everything, great and small, from the moment life lays it at their feet. The tough times are valuable lessons, and everything else, each as a gift to value and appreciate. By this, every moment is a new gift, and everything becomes more than enough.

So what is the great lesson and the greatest way to teach this most valuable way of living life? Not just by word, but more importantly by our own personal demonstrations. What they see us value, they come to value. How we express our gratitude, they too learn what and how to express. As our thank-full hearts grow, theirs grow as well. As we learn, live and demonstrate a lifestyle that places no conditions on our happiness, a life of appreciation, they to learn what a happy life is really all about.

## *Day 134*

**If we're not happy with what we have, why would we think we'll be happy with more?**

Once we've learned the lesson of appreciation, once we're thankful for all we have, then the Universe says, "Now you're ready for more."

## *Day 135*

**Planning is good, being overly attached to our plans is not.**

Be willing to change your plans as you go along. The Spiritual path unfolds before us from moment to moment, be open to it.

## *Day 136*

**Faith is giving thanks for a good day, first thing in the morning.**

Start this day off right, connect with Goodness, and start with an attitude of thankful appreciation.

## _Day 137_

**Today is a Good day; as Good as you allow it to be.**

Trust the natural unfolding of events; allow this day to flow as is. Forcing anything causes friction, the friction of what you want rubbing up against what is to be. Instead surrender to the natural flow of life, see where it takes you, its purpose is Good, its ways most pleasant. Enjoy.

## _Day 138_

**Is change good or bad?**

Resist change, refuse to accept it, and it's bad. Allow change, accepting it just as it unfolds, and it's Good. It's all up to you. Choose well.

## _Day 139_

**The way from lack to abundance is a 3 part path.**

That path is one of Action, Faith, and Appreciation.

## _Day 140_

**Wisdom knows nothing.**

The most valuable thing I know is that I don't know it all. This is the beginning of true wisdom.

## _Day 141_

**Would you like you if you met you?**

Become the kind of person you'd prefer to be around.

Alone or not, be in Good company.

## _Day 142_

**Happiness isn't something we find, it's something we tune into.**

How?

Gratitude and Appreciation. Acknowledge the Good in your life right now. Tune in.

## *Day 143*

**Change is possible, even when you find you're dissatisfied with a seemingly unchangeable situation.**

This change is to change your mental and emotional relation to the situation. This can be done simply by either changing your expectations on how you think things should be, or accepting things just as they already are. These two changes are always an option.

## *Day 144*

**New day, New Experiences.**

A continual renewing of one's spiritual practices opens new channels, awakens new understandings and ignites new joys. Try something new and different this week. Start today.

## _Day 145_

**New beginnings are often disguised as painful endings.**

Most Good change begins with a bit of discomfort, so let it be a sign of Good things to come.

## _Day 146_

**The same door through which one gives, one also receives.**

Open the door.

## _Day 147_

**One for the agenda.**

Consider adding to your agenda today, at least one positive contribution to the wellbeing of another. A lifting word or an outward act of kindness.

## _Day 148_

**The best gifts we can give:**

Our time, our attention, our Love, and our forgiveness.

## _Day 149_

**Seek first to understand, listen more, talk less.**

Remember, a verbal response isn't always necessary, an accepting nod and a smile usually says so much more.

## _Day 150_

**Change is natural and inevitable, simple, and easy.**

It's our resistance to change that hurts. Once we stop grasping and clinging, and begin letting go, change gets easier and starts making sense.

## _Day 151_

**Seek to see the miracles and the lessons in every encounter and every situation.**

By this simple consistent practice, we tune into an awareness of God-in-action.

## _Day 152_

**Wisdom isn't knowing, it's knowing you don't.**

Lay aside criticism, pride and stubbornness.

Be a student, teachable and willing to consider other points of view.

## _Day 153_

**Take care not to get hung up on words and miss the meaning they're giving.**

Old Zen Saying: Take care not to fixate on the finger pointing at the moon, missing the moon itself.

Words are but sign posts, labels. Has the world and other people's views defined the meaning of certain words for you? Let go of these labels and come to know these things as they really are, to you. Spiritual masters meet here, behind the words.

## _Day 154_

**Today is a gift.**

Some won't wake up today; some of us may not tomorrow. Today is a priceless gift, there will never be another exactly like it, cherish it, enjoy it.

## _Day 155_

### "I'll just figure it out."

Figuring it out? Thinking our way out of fear or anxiety doesn't work, it only adds fuel to the fire. Take care not to get caught up in this snowballing trap. Stop over thinking it and focus on the present moment instead, once settled a bit, rest in this state for a while, staying present, at least until the negative emotions subside. They will. Trust the process.

## _Day 156_

### Losing hope?

A loss in hope doesn't mean hope is really lost. It's not a change in reality, only a change in one's perception. Hope doesn't get lost, only temporarily forgotten. Whether you're seeing it or not, the truth is, there is Hope. It's not lost.

## _Day 157_

**Place your hand over your heart, feel that?**

That's called purpose.

If ever you doubt having purpose, feel your heart;

it beats for a reason and a purpose.

## _Day 158_

**If today was your last day…**

If today was your last, what would you want to be

remembered for tomorrow?

"What can I do today to bring happiness to

others?"

It's a very nice way to live.

## _Day 159_

**Nothing is lost, it only changes form.**

Remember, beneath all things, it is The

Universe/God that is your ultimate and unfailing supply.

## _Day 160_

**Don't let success go to your head or failure to your heart.**

Keep from these extremes; take care not to get overly attached to either.

Practice balance.

## _Day 161_

**We meet no ordinary people in our lives.**

For each person you meet, pay attention and learn their purpose in your life, and yours in theirs. They're all intricate and valuable encounters.

## _Day 162_

**Justice**

It's not that the Universe isn't Just, it's that we can't fully comprehend how Divine justice works.

Trust the Divine, and ultimately Good prevails.

Just Trust.

## Day 163

**Just be.**

When we let go and allow, we become who we are meant to be. Follow a Good path, but allow The Universe to determine each next step. Let go, Let God.

## Day 164

**Plug into your source of Good.**

Take the time daily to reconnect, to stay connected.

A few moments of silence and stillness can pleasantly transform your day.

## Day 165

**It's ok to be ok with letting it be.**

Life seems better when things are going our way, yet life is best once this no longer matters.

Replace your need to control with Faith. It'll serve you well.

## _Day 166_

**Let go.**

As we continually let go of our preconceived ideas and expectations, from moment to moment, our attention awakens, our vision clears, and a new and wonderful world begins coming into view.

## _Day 167_

**Need answers?**

Have a question? Get still and quiet, and then ask the part of you that knows.

There is Power and Wisdom in Stillness and Silence.

Take the time daily just to be still and listen.

## _Day 168_

**When having a bad day.**

You can start your day over at any point you'd like. Simply close your eyes, take a deep breath, say a prayer, and begin again.

Enjoy your day!

## _Day 169_

**What are you?**

I was asked recently, "Are you a taker or are you a giver?"

## _Day 170_

**Don't say it, do it!**

Criticizing how something is being done wrong helps nothing, try instead promoting and demonstrating what is right.

Don't live in the problem, live the solution.

## _Day 171_

**Finding the solution.**

Owning our feelings rather than blaming them on somebody else is the best position we can take in resolving our upset. For then our solution rests now within our reach, within us, not out there with them, completely out of our control.

The solution always rests with the real problem, not the alleged one.

## _Day 172_

**Know**

To acquire knowledge, one must study; but to acquire wisdom, one must openly observe. Stay Teachable.

## _Day 173_

**Have an idea of how your day is going to go?**

Let that go, so to see what really happens.

## _Day 174_

**The Forgiver wins!**

Give the first five people who allegedly do you wrong today permission to be wrong, giving yourself a five person buffer between your being upset and your being at peace.

## _Day 175_

**True Happiness is unconditional.**

Let go of the "if onlys."

The conditions we place on our happiness are the only real things between us and it.

## _Day 176_

**When the water gets muddy, give it time to clear before getting back in.**

Before acting or reacting, strongly consider first giving it some time, letting go, detaching, and then later revisiting the matter with a clearer more grounded perspective. From this place we are more apt to take a sensible, intuitively influenced, and well balanced action, or maybe find it best to take no action at all. Be patient with yourself, the situation, and always place peace first and last.

## _Day 177_

**Everything will be OK only when we are OK with everything.**

Consider the hands-off approach, adjusting your attitude instead.

## _Day 178_

**Crunching life now so you might relax one day?**

Isn't today a "one day" too? Make your "one days" now, many and, in between, rather than one day far and long away.

## _Day 179_

**Criticizing doesn't reveal the criticized; it reveals the criticizer.**

Don't be one. There are better ways to feel equal. When you feel less than, lift others up. When you feel more than, lift others up.

## _Day 180_

**For comfort and peace, keep from the extremes in life, good or bad.**

Focus on balance and Stay Centered.

## *Day 181*

**A Gratitude Walk.**

Try this: Take a short walk outside, and saying "Thank You" for everything you see or think of; your shoes, the sky, the grass, the air your breathing, your lungs, your hands, a tree, whatever comes in sight or to mind.

A 15 minute walk like this is guaranteed to lift you up.

Take as needed.


## *Day 182*

**Open-mindedness**

Spiritual growth is a process of letting go of the old, making room for the new; Ideas, methods, beliefs, and attitudes.

## _Day 183_

**Be sure to add "Just relax a little" to your list of things to do today.**

Make time to do nothing, simply relax, and be present.

## _Day 184_

**It's an inside job.**

Rather than strenuously attempting to adjust the events or circumstances of your life, especially those out of your reach, adjust instead your faith, fears and desires, all well within your reach.

## _Day 185_

**Life is guaranteed to give lessons, yet learning is optional.**

Embrace life's lessons and you'll come to know each one's meaning and Good purpose.

## _Day 186_

**Forget what is wrong; pay attention to what is right.**

It has much more to offer.

## _Day 187_

**Today is a Good day; as Good as you allow it to be.**

Trust the natural unfolding of events; allow this day to flow as is. Forcing anything causes friction, the friction of what you want rubbing up against what is to be. Instead Surrender to the natural flow of life, see where it takes you, its purpose is Good, its ways most pleasant.

## _Day 188_

**Practice Patience**

Patience isn't having the ability to wait, it's an attitude one takes while waiting. One that says, "I'm ok with just being present," fully taking in what this moment has to offer, not rushing life, but instead trusting its natural flow. Practice Patience.

## _Day 189_

**Pay attention to the chance encounters, coincidences, the people you meet, the things you hear and see. They all have a message for you.**

When the student is ready, the teachers, the lessons, will appear. Be ready, alert, and pay attention.

## _Day 190_

**Practice seeing all as interconnected, all as equal and all as growing into an understanding of its present realized full potential.**

Everyone is at the place they are in their growth that is just right for them. Accept this. None are better than others; they are simply just where they're meant to be. We all are connected in many ways, inside and out. See others in yourself and yourself in others.

## _Day 191_

**Acceptance changes things.**

Acceptance doesn't just give us a better perspective; it gives us a clearer picture, better situating us for proper and sane action.

## _Day 192_

**When stressfully pushing for your way, to make your point or win, pause and consider this:**

"How important is this compared to my having peace?"

## _Day 193_

**It's not the load that breaks us down, it's in the way we carry it.**

A Good attitude carries a lot of weight.

## _Day 194_

**Relax**

Give yourself permission to suspend over-thinking, planning or fixing, just for today. Allow yourself a day of mental rest and relaxation.

This will serve you well.

## _Day 195_

**We are rarely upset for the reason we think and we are most usually better than we think we are.**

Don't believe everything you think. Think less.

## _Day 196_

**Not forgiving is just our turn to be wrong**.

Forgiveness isn't about letting anyone off the hook; it's about letting you off the hook.

Be Free.

## _Day 197_

**It's not what we don't know that can hurt us.**

What's dangerous is our knowing things for sure that aren't so.

Be willing to challenge your own points of view.

## _Day 198_

**Worry doesn't change the outcome, it only ruins the journey.**

To better affect an outcome, give your all to the present moment, mentally and spiritually. When you do get to where you're headed, then you'll be ready, for however things turn out, in a much better state of mind and spirit to accept the outcome.

## _Day 199_

**Want to see clearly? Close your eyes and open your heart.**

When in question, simply ask the part of you that knows. Pray about it, put it out of mind for a while, and then return to the question in meditation.

With practice, and an honest interpretation of the answer, you will receive the answer directing you in the interest of your highest Good, and the highest Good of all involved.

## _Day 200_

### Humility vs. Pride

Humility, the door to awakening, shares no space

or thought with its weak

shadow called pride.

Humility, seeing ourselves as equal to all is an

acknowledgment of our

connectedness with each other and our God, bringing

forth an experience of trust in

the process of life and a relaxed perception and

acceptance of change. Pride, seeing

ourselves better or less than others is an illusion of

separateness that breeds only

loneliness and seclusion.

## _Day 201_

**Giving up the blame game.**

When a negative situation arises, honestly try to see how you're

playing a part in either keeping the ill alive inside yourself or the situation outside

yourself. We should watch for fear and self-centeredness. The more we do this with ourselves, the more we will understand the silliness in the blame game.

## _Day 202_

**If you let go of what you might be, you may be pleased with who you are**.

If you let go of striving to receive, you will receive just what you need.

## _Day 203_

**Until we are emptied of the old, there is no room for the new.**

For a new perspective, simply let go of the one you hold now and your new one will come into view. No need to try and figure anything else out. Simply Surrender.

## _Day 204_

**Stressing a decision? Not sure what to do?**

Let it go for a while. We are blinded by our grasping and stressing, it clouds our vision. Let go first, even if just for a little while, and you'll find when you will return to it, (if you even do), you'll have a much clearer picture of what's best to do.

## _Day 205_

**Spiritual Truths**

There is strength in softness, power in flexibility, perfection in mistakes, success in failure, clarity in confusion, and love in letting go.

## _Day 206_

**Anything is Possible.**

Don't be discouraged by your human limitations, for your true nature, being spiritual, always has direct access to the unlimited wisdom and power of the Divine. All things are possible when we come from our unlimited source of Good.

## *Day 207*

**Do you listen to your favorite song in anticipation for the end, or do you enjoy it each moment all the way through?**

Do the same with each day. Your day is your song, cherish each note, each moment, for enjoyment of the whole.

## *Day 208*

**As gratitude grows, fears slip away and abundance unfolds**

Practice appreciation.

## *Day 209*

**When feeling upset that something isn't going the way you want...**

... simply shift your focus from "What's in it for me?" to "How may I serve?"

## *Day 210*

**Life's lessons; we can prolong them, but we can't avoid them.**

The only way to end a lesson is to learn that lesson.

Be willing to face them and to learn them.

## *Day 211*

**We all have our rough edges.**

It's when the rough edges of others rub up against ours that we must remember, it's a Good thing, it's a natural part of the "smoothing out of our rough edges" process.

## *Day 212*

**Take some time today to rekindle your spiritual connection.**

Try a new prayer, a new meditation, a new mantra, take a quiet walk in the woods, sit on the beach watching the waves. Whatever deeply connects you.

## _Day 213_

**Our four greatest teachers:**

Nature, children, our mistakes, and the mistakes
of others.

## _Day 214_

**Practice living in a state of present moment
appreciation, openly aware of and acknowledging the
gifts Life is placing right before you.**

By doing this your gratitude will begin to expand,
and you'll come to know the true meaning of
thankfulness.

## _Day 215_

**What's lacking in any relationship is but what we're
not giving**.

Strive to give, rather than to get, and you'll
receive in great measure.

## _Day 216_

**Be positive, wherever you are.**

When looking back, look with a heart full of thanks, when looking ahead, look with a mind full of hope, but whenever possible just stay present, keeping a heart and mind full of appreciation.

## _Day 217_

**Getting involved in a problem only feeds it**.

Half of most problems are our struggling with the problem. The first step in problem solving is letting it go.

## _Day 218_

**Everyone can be your teacher.**

In the practice of unconditional love and tolerance, one's alleged enemy is really their best teacher.

## _Day 219_

**Trade your limitations for inspirations.**

Rather than discussing what's wrong, or what could go wrong, look for and discuss what's right, and what could go right, and by this, it most likely will.

## _Day 220_

**All of Creation extends teachings of understanding, lessons for the betterment of our lives.**

Utilize this gift. Pay attention, be open, and remain teachable - it will serve you well.

## _Day 221_

**We experience our day not by the circumstances of it, but through the filter of our outlook upon it.**

Circumstances can't always be changed, but our outlook can. Choose a Good one and have a Good day.

## _Day 222_

**Happiness isn't something we find, it's something we tune into.**

How? Gratitude and Appreciation. Acknowledge the Good in your life right now.

Tune in.

## _Day 223_

**Take care not to worry about what you may lose or may never get, or anguish over what you have lost or never had, for by this we miss the crown jewel, the awareness of the gifts we have right now**.

Ignore the temptation to focus on the past or the future, keep your thoughts on what you have in your life today, right now. Appreciate it and give thanks for it and enjoy a life of genuine gratitude.

## *Day 224*

**Where the Spirit guides, It provides**.

If The Divine brings you to it, it'll get you through it. The Universe always finishes what It has begun; Its purpose? Your Ultimate Highest Good.

## *Day 225*

**Positive thinking**

Negative thoughts can be drowned out and eventually replaced by using repetitive Positive affirmations.

"All is well,"

"I trust God,"

"It all has Good purpose,"

"I am healthy, whole and blessed."

It works with practice.

## *Day 226*

**To the degree that we let go of doubt do we allow The Miraculous to come about.**

Believe it and you'll see it.

## *Day 227*

**See yourself in others and others in yourself.**

Point out similarities, dismiss differences.

Promote Unity, Understanding, and Compassion.

These will serve you well.

## *Day 228*

**When we serve others, we are serving the purposes of a Grand design, a Design which includes the quickest possible unfolding of our own highest good**.

Serve Well.

## _Day 229_

**Change is possible when you find you're dissatisfied with an unchangeable situation.**

Change your mental and emotional relation to the situation. This can be done simply by either changing your expectations on how you think things should be, or accepting things just as they already are.

## _Day 230_

**Finding a Truth is good, losing an illusion is better.**

The Spiritual journey isn't as much one of discovering the new as it is one of discarding the old. Finding your misperceptions and misunderstandings is a great victory; it is the first step to fresh and new understandings and awakenings. Always welcome new points of view, with a willingness to happily discard yours.

## _Day 231_

**First things first:**

Be mindful of your priorities, choosing Good ones as first, and continually redirecting yourself in their direction.

## _Day 232_

**Break the habit.**

Worry is a bad habit of thinking, and can be broken. Replace it with a new habit, a habit of faithful anticipation. It may be a challenge at first, but it works.

## _Day 233_

**Everyone is your teacher.**

Everyone is a teacher, teaching us what to do, or what not to do, showing us how we'd like to be, or don't want to be. Everyone has a lesson for us.

## _Day 234_

**Some good characteristics are only developed by trying times, some prayers only answered through challenging situations.**

After prayer, it all has Good purpose.

## _Day 235_

**Be mindful of the power of your faith.**

Do you power fear, faith in discord, or do you power hope, faith in Goodness and order? Put your faith in what works for you, not against you.

## _Day 236_

**It's been told by the great masters in many different ways, it's one of the great inescapable governing spiritual laws:**

"What we serve to others, the Universe will serve to us in return."

Take care and choose well.

## _Day 237_

**The Universe does not withhold Good.**

The Good that you deeply desire, may not come at the time or in the way you're expecting, but it's already on its way, in fact it probably is already here. Keep watch where you usually wouldn't, expect it in ways you might not even understand, and simply Trust.

## _Day 238_

**It has purpose.**

One day you'll look back on your life and see that most every time you thought you were being rejected from something good, you were actually being redirected to something better.

## _Day 239_

**Appreciation multiplies the appreciated and awakens the appreciator.**

Consciously acknowledge the gifts in your life right now. Live in thankfulness.

## _Day 240_

**When stressed or overwhelmed...**

If in a stressful situation, step back and look at the big picture, while keeping in mind, this too shall pass. If feeling overwhelmed, look at the small picture, by coming back into the present moment, while keeping in mind, first things first.

## _Day 241_

**See unity.**

Consider this, rather than looking for differences between others and yourself, recognize the similarities. One creates loneliness, the other emotional security.

## _Day 242_

**Consider this for today:**

If you feel the urge to criticize or complain, compliment and say something positive instead. Simple, not always easy, but very rewarding and very Good.

## _Day 243_

**Ego repels, Humility attracts.**

People are naturally drawn to those who lift others up, rather than those who glorify themselves. Take care and choose well.

## _Day 244_

**Be Free.**

Anger is a cage, the bars of its cage are blame, self-centeredness, and self-pity. Remember, justifying anger is only protecting your prison. Be free.

## Day 245

**Turn from the problem.**

The depth of one's anxiety measures the quality of one's spiritual condition.

Don't struggle with your problems, connect with the Solution instead.

## Day 246

**If something isn't meant to be, it won't, and if it is, it will.**

Maybe instead of trying to change things, we might just practice a little acceptance instead.

## Day 247

**Let go of the need to defend yourself.**

Only pride needs defense, why defend pride? The part of you that deserves your attention needs no defense, focus there.

## *Day 248*

**When you feel you've exhausted all possibilities, remember this: You haven't.**

Tune in to your source of Good, reconnect, relax, and simply begin again.

## *Day 249*

**Our first step in resolving anger is to not take the actions of others personally; it always has more to do with them than it does you.**

The next is to find the part you played, whether it's actually in the situation, or whether it's within yourself, your fears, expectations, or prejudices. Admitting our part is our first step in resolving the situation and our first step toward peace.

## _Day 250_

**The solution can't be found at the same level as the problem.**

When a problem comes, first step back, let it go for a while, put your thoughts on something Positive for a bit. By this you'll be more clear-minded and emotionally centered, better equipped to see the solution. In fact, by this, many times we find that this was itself the solution: simply letting go.

## _Day 251_

**Have an open mind.**

If you want to continue to grow, always question your perceptions, and always be willing to change your mind.

## Day 252

**It's better to make use of a chance to change rather than try to change the chance.**

Change is inevitable, but change is Good, when we allow it. Allow it.

## Day 253

**If speech is silver, silence is gold.**

When you must speak, speak just a few words, kind and soft.

Want to be heard? This is the way to reach a listener's ear.

## Day 254

**Does everything happen for a reason?**

Maybe those who can't say everything happens for a good reason will one day see that everything that does happen can be made to have a Good purpose.

## _Day 255_

**We get what we give.**

Consider showing others the same respect, kindness, forgiveness, and understanding, that you'd expect others to give you. You'll get what you give. Choose well.

## _Day 256_

**Imperfection is perfect.**

Low self-esteem and insecurities often arise from one's need to be seen as, or to be, perfect. Let this go and just be you. Only then will you truly feel secure.

## _Day 257_

**Love and tolerance tires out its opposition.**

Love others until they can learn to love themselves.

## _Day 258_

**Being wrong can be right.**

Rejoice when finding that you've been wrong, for you have just learned something new, and you're a bit wiser now than you were yesterday.

## _Day 259_

**Ask frequently.**

A good question to often ask oneself: "What could be the purpose of this person in my life, what am I to teach them, or they to teach me?"

## _Day 260_

**Count your blessings.**

Don't count your problems, count your blessings, no matter how small they at first may seem, for what we look for, the more of which we will see. Choose well.

## _Day 261_

### Change the focus.

Here's an example: Let's say you're complaining that your back is hurting. Be sure to acknowledge that your arms, legs, and feet don't, your lungs are clear, your heart is pumping, and your eyes can see, and even give a prayer of thanks for those things.

Positive thinking is a habit that needs to be developed by practice.

## _Day 262_

### What do you Trust in?

Trust fear? How many times have our fears actually come true, especially to the extent we've imagined? So why do we continue to trust fear? Don't! Fear tells us that if we put our guard down we'll get hurt, the truth is it's the fear itself that hurts.

When we put our guard down, and let go of fear, we have peace.

Don't trust fear, it lies. Choose peace instead.

## _Day 263_

**Be careful not to defeat yourself by being an all or nothing person.**

It's not about how far you're getting, it's that you're moving, and in the right direction.

## _Day 264_

**A bend in the road is not the end of the road, unless you fail to make the turn.**

Consider allowing rather than resisting. Choose Peace over conflict

## _Day 265_

**Happiness doesn't come by getting what we want; it awakens while appreciating what we have.**

Use today to take notice and better cherish the gifts in your life.

## _Day 266_

**Morning gratitude short list:**

1. Woke up

2. Roof over head

3. Food to eat

4. Air to breathe

It's a Good day.


## _Day 267_

**"Should have"s and "shouldn't have"s are a waste of time, they serve no good purpose and keep you stuck in the past.**

Make your amends, make your apologies, forgive, learn from it, and move on.

## _Day 268_

**Life gives lessons, and not always in ways we'd agree with or expect.**

But its purpose is Good, its goal, your peace.

Be teachable and open as a student of life.


## _Day 269_

**People will naturally tend to treat us the way we treat them and the way they see us treating others**.

We have more control over how others treat us than we may think.

Simply treat others as you would like to be treated.

Kindness invites kindness.

## Day 270

**The answers to prayer.**

God answers prayers in one of three ways: yes,
no, or not just yet.


## Day 271

**The greatest gift one can give oneself is to give of
oneself.**

Giving - the best form of self-help.
Servant-- the highest and most rewarding position
in the spiritual community.


## Day 272

**To trust that purpose and meaning can arise from any
adversity is to live a life of comfort.**

You begin to understand that no situation is
exempt from the unfolding and healing processes of
Good.

## *Day 273*

**People take things as they are, not necessarily as it is given.**

People react according to their expectations and current attitudes.

Don't take it personally.


## *Day 274*

**Don't look back; you're not going that way.**

What matters most isn't where you are or where you were, but rather, that you are moving and the direction in which you are headed.


## *Day 275*

**Rather than grieving what you've lost, be thankful for the blessing of having had it.**

By letting go of the old we're making room for the new.

## _Day 276_

**Acceptance begins with the willingness to accept.**

Start here by saying aloud: "I can't seem to accept this. But to accept this, I am willing."

## _Day 277_

**Watch your words.**

The words we use are either contributing to a Positive attitude or negative attitude, a Good day or a bad one. Choose well.

## _Day 278_

**Bumps in the road often occur to knock us back on track.**

By these unexpected, and seemingly unwanted, changes, we are guided and redirected toward our Highest Good.

## _Day 279_

**The Universe has big plans for you.**

Your part? Make yourself ready; Be Teachable,
Flexible, Open-minded, and Forgiving.

Freeing yourself up for Positive change.


## _Day 280_

**You are fully equipped for anything that may stand
before you today**.

All that is required was built into you at birth.
Trust in the Wisdom that created you.

## _Day 281_

**The two ways to get enough:**

There are two ways to get enough.

One is to accumulate more. The other is to desire
less.

Yet eventually one comes to know this Truth;
enough isn't a goal one reaches, it's a God-given
Wholeness one realizes.

You're enough.

## _Day 282_

**Start thinking of what is right.**

Today, when tempted to focus on what is wrong,
pay attention to what is right.

It has much more to offer.

## _Day 283_

**Try This…**

Take two pieces of small paper. Write on one, "See the lesson in this." And on the second, "Forget what's wrong, pay attention to what's right."

Now put one in each of your front pockets.

You'll forget about them, and then stumble upon them right when you need them. During the day, when you pull one out, stop and see how it applies to your current situation.


## _Day 284_

**Don't label your life situations.**

"This is bad," "this is good." Avoid this.

Avoid judging your life situations, it limits the possibilities.

Instead, relax your resistance, knowing that the Divine is continually working for your highest Good.

## _Day 285_

**Obstacles hide possibilities.**

One's next obstacle is one's next reward simply in disguise.

## _Day 286_

**Commit this day to lifting others up.**

Speak words of encouragement, compliment them, point out their positive qualities, and make them smile.

The more we can see these good things in others, the more we see them in ourselves.

Lift and be lifted.

## _Day 287_

**The wise often say, "I don't know."**

There is wisdom in not knowing all the answers and a freedom in knowing you don't have to.

## _Day 288_

**The JOY is in the Journey.**

As you move today, be present and take it slow so as not to miss the countless subtle gifts popping up along the way.

## _Day 289_

**Every experience is but a necessary step on your path**

Take care not to get hung up on any one step along the way, Good or bad. Simply let it come. And then let it go. As we discard the old, we make way for the new.

Make yourself ready. The Universe has great plans for you.

## _Day 290_

**It's all Good.**

Seemingly impossible situations serve their purpose too, for they force us to look for possibilities beyond ourselves.

This is usually a lesson we've long been avoiding.

## _Day 291_

**From the Right perspective, it all makes sense.**

Faith, humility, love, and selflessness reveal this perspective.

## Day 292

**Quiet the mind.**

Take time to get quiet. Turn off all sound and give yourself at least a few moments to just sit and be present.

Start now.

## _Day 293_

**It's OK.**

It's OK not to be perfect. In fact, it feels pretty nice. Keep this in mind today.

Just be.

## _Day 294_

**Empty Yourself.**

We have no more room for more when full. For continued spiritual growth, every so often, lay aside all your understandings and beliefs, and begin again.

## Day 295

**_You_ be.**

Be the person you'd like to be around, do the things you'd like to see others do.

## _Day 296_

**They're watching.**

Your life is your lesson. Teach well.

## _Day 297_

**Always a solution.**

Prayer is always an option. Sometimes just one simple prayer is all it takes.

## _Day 298_

**In need?**

Give first. Focus on giving.

## _Day 299_

**Your focus is your experience.**

Take care not to spend too much time focusing on what you don't have. Over-focusing on "not having" only attracts more "not having" into your life. Focus on having, and more and more will begin to appear.

## _Day 300_

**Thank God?**

What if you woke up tomorrow with only the things you thanked God for today? Give thanks.

## _Day 301_

**Affirmations**

Remember the tool of positive affirmations:

"I am well."

"Prosperity and abundance flows into my life."

"The Universe is my unfailing supply."

"I am happy and free."

Say these 10 times each, or more. Use your own,
use them daily.

## _Day 302_

**That thing you've been putting off?**

To have something you've never had you've got
to do something you've never done.

Take action today.

## _Day 303_

**Choose peace.**

Give the first seven people who allegedly do you wrong today permission to be wrong, giving yourself a seven person buffer between you being upset or you being at peace.

## _Day 304_

**Gratitude**

Gratitude is a habit, just like worry is a habit. Spend time consciously cultivating the habit of appreciation. Continually count your blessings, even the ones you don't see yet.

## _Day 305_

**Be you.**

People are drawn to, attracted to and happy to be around, those who are simply themselves. No matter how different you may feel at times, if you're just yourself, people know, if you're not, people know.

## _Day 306_

**Take care on what you let in.**

Pay attention to how you feel while listening to certain music, watching certain TV or movies, doing certain things, being around certain people.

Now Choose peace and live accordingly.

## _Day 307_

**For greatest strength and power:**

Be gentle, subtle, kind, careful, and humble.

## _Day 308_

**The Power in Letting Go.**

Once we choose the path of Surrender, of letting go, personal limitations and weaknesses no longer matter, for now something Greater is at work, through us.

## _Day 309_

**Acceptance**

Accepting an unwanted situation doesn't mean you're settling for less.

Acceptance is your first step in changing or letting go of the situation. We cannot move forward until we first know where we stand. Acceptance gives us a clear picture of where we are. Acceptance is to come fully into the place we are, physically, mentally, or however our relation is to the situation. It's putting the option of choice back into our hands. It's simply saying, "OK, I see, this is how it is, it is what it is." And now you're at the place to do something about it.

Non-acceptance is a denial of reality; acceptance is a step into Truth.

## _Day 310_

### Appreciation

We could stand in a dark room with all the riches of the world around us and never even know.

Appreciation is the result of the casting of the light of our attention on the blessings in our lives.

Pay attention to what counts, count your blessings. Make appreciation a habit, through daily practice, and your world comes alive, and full of riches.

## _Day 311_

**Take notice and give thanks.**

Practice seeing and taking notice of the small blessings: a small flower in a patch of weeds, a ray of sunlight, a bird song, the sound of the wind in the trees, a friendly smile, a loving touch, a child's giggle, a bird on the windowsill, your heartbeat.

Take notice and say a silent thank you for these gifts and a silent thank you to these gifts for their presence in your life.

## _Day 312_

**Kindness**

Those who seek to find ways to be extra kind, find that extra kindness comes to them.

Try this today and see what happens.

## *Day 313*

### Love

It's easy to love those we like, but what about those we don't, and why would we anyways? There may be someone who doesn't like us, yet they're accepting of us, unconditionally loving us.

Love means, I accept you're as imperfect as I am, someone who wants security and acceptance, someone who may be scared and shows it in the wrong ways, someone who is as worthy of my understanding, love, and acceptance as may feel I am of theirs. Someone who needs someone to love them first.

## *Day 314*

### Peace

When frustrated, in a confrontation or being stubborn, ask yourself this, "How important is this compared to my having peace?"

Choosing otherwise is a loss.

Choose peace.

## *Day 315*

### Quiet and Still

Make it a regular routine to have time to sit quiet and still, being present.

Look at something present with you to help keep your mind occupied and present: a plant, a tree, a picture.

The body rests: the mind needs rest too.

## _Day 316_

### Honesty

Honesty, with self, is the safety net keeping one from a fall into ignorance, ill-perception, and self-deceit. Practice honesty.

## _Day 317_

### Open-Mindedness

The more open, the more we see. But how?

Always honestly consider other points of view; continually question your points of view, occasionally discard old ideas and understandings. Don't miss the message because of a dislike of the messenger or the way the message is carried.

Seek to see anew. It keeps life interesting, alive, and full of possibilities.

## _Day 318_

### Action

What we do speaks much louder than what we say. The fact that we are doing it or not, speaks the loudest.

Take action, or not, but do what you'd say you'd do. Do what is right.

Do it today.


## _Day 319_

### Apology

That one you've been putting off, its time.

Make your apology today, or make the first step toward it.

## _Day 320_

### Humility

To see yourself in others and others in yourself.

Whether we see it or not, we are all equal. The more we can learn to see this, the more life becomes our friend.

## _Day 321_

### Making Amends

An apology is just that: an uttering of words. Yet in order for an apology to be authentic, it must be followed by a change in the apologizer.

The apology is but the starting line, the amends continue for the rest of our lives.

## _Day 322_

**Pray for the Willingness.**

Every action is preceded by a thought. Every thought for action is preceded by willingness or a desire.

For a desired personal action, change or state of mind, pray for the willingness, even if you must first pray for the willingness to be willing.

## _Day 323_

**Be aware of your thoughts and actions.**

Continually be aware of your motives, your actions, where you may owe an apology, something you know you must do. Watch for envy, jealousy, anger, or greed. These are problems that begin and end only within us. They are poisons that destroy one from the inside out.

Stay right with yourself and others.

Keep yourself right with the world and the world will be right with you.


## _Day 324_

**Pray**

Say a prayer at the top of every hour today. The best prayers: prayers for others and prayers of thanks.

## _Day 325_

### Meditate

If you don't have one already, start a regular routine of meditation. You will soon see that nothing more affects your day than the time you've spent in meditation.

Start simple and keep it simple.

## _Day 326_

### Serve

Try to enjoy the fruits of the selfless.

Today, echo this saying in your head all day, and act accordingly: "How may I serve...How may I serve...How may I serve?"

## _Day 327_

**Which comes first, Cause or Effect?**

Remember, it's not what happens to us that causes our state of mind: it's our state of mind that determines the experiences we have.

## _Day 328_

**Trust**

Trust in the Wisdom and Love of the one who created you.

## _Day 329_

**Let Go.**

Surrender this day. Continually let go, from moment to moment. Live a day of non-resistance. Trust the natural flow of life.

When frustrated or stressed, step back, take a breath, and begin again.

Simply surrender.

# _Day 330_

## Positive Affirmations

Say them aloud. Use throughout the day,
especially first thing in the morning.

-Today is a good day and all things are possible.

- My good is unlimited and continually manifests.

- Joy is my natural state of being.

- Miracles are unfolding for me and those around me in
each present moment.

- There is an abundant supply for every need.

- I'm a channel of Universal Love and Light.

- I give thanks that all my good manifests now in a
perfect way.

- All that is happening is happening for a Good purpose.

## _Day 331_

**Positive Affirmations**

More for today. Come up with some of your own.

- All is well, all is well, all is well.

- Full prosperity comes to me in perfect ways.

- I am Joyful and full of light and I see the Light in others.

- Perfect health is my constant state of being.

- God works continually for my highest good.

- I live a life with harmonious relationships.

- God is with me and sustains me.

- Perfect understanding and Trust in God are mine.

- I attract and draw into my life good people, peaceful circumstance and overflowing abundance.

## _Day 332_

### Stay Present

Take care not to waste your present moments thinking, discussing, or trying to rewrite yesterday or over planning, rushing or impatiently awaiting the tomorrow.

Value and live your moments, one by one.

## _Day 333_

### Be the example

The most influence we can have on others is in being a good example.

Be first as you'd wish others to be.

## _Day 334_

### Negate the negative, perpetuate the Positive.

Distance yourself from the negative, focus on the positive.

## _Day 335_

**Life is a gift.**

Every heartbeat, every breath, every friendly smile, every lesson, every challenge, every victory.


## _Day 336_

**The key to reaching a goal:**

1. Set the goal.

2. Take the first step.

3. Continue, one step at a time.

The Big Rule: Keep your eye on the goal and the next step only.

## *Day 337*

### It's just ahead...or is it?

The treasure is often found on the pathway to the
treasure chest.

Many times the treasure is the pathway itself,
many times the journey.

Don't miss the joy of the present moment by
looking too far ahead.

The rewards are always given in the present.


## *Day 338*

### Expect great things.

A key in bringing abundance into your life by is
living in a state of abundance. This is done through
expecting abundance and trusting that it is now flowing
into your life. By this practice we tune ourselves to see it.

We see it, and then see it more and more.

Affirmation: "Thank you for the abundance and
prosperity flowing into my life right now."

Say it over and over, and then pay attention.

## _Day 339_

### Life

It's not a challenge to be met; it's a reality to be experienced. Don't take things so seriously.

Laugh at yourself often. Help others to lighten up as well.

## _Day 340_

### Remember, bad situations always look different later.

Remember this when in a "bad situation": This too shall pass and it's not as serious as it looks right now.

## _Day 341_

**The power of a thought.**

One positive change in thinking, one positive thought, even just the willingness to step out of a mental pattern, is enough to change your whole day, possibly your life.

Every thought is like a pebble thrown into a pond, its effects ripple out throughout your life.

Take care and choose well.

## _Day 342_

**Morning Prayer and Meditation Time**

If you're not already doing daily, morning, prayer and meditation, please do.

Make a commitment to give yourself 15 minutes each morning for connecting with the Divine, doing positive affirmations, reading something positive, prayer, and meditation.

All of these or just a few, but begin with 15 minutes for one or two weeks. Once you've seen the powerful effects, extend your commitment and your time in the morning.

## _Day 343_

**Set and reset your priorities.**

Continually re-determine your priorities. Set them and continually readjust as you go along. Don't beat yourself up for falling short. Just simply step back on track and proceed.

## _Day 344_

**It's time.**

If you're waiting for the perfect time and it's not coming, change your idea of perfect.

## _Day 345_

**Not things.**

Remember, it is gratitude and appreciation that lifts us up. Not things.

It is appreciation and thankfulness that makes us feel secure. Not things.

It is gratitude and thankfulness that is priceless. Not things.


## _Day 346_

**Change is good.**

Embrace change. Trust Change. Accept change today.

## _Day 347_

**Change is the only constant.**

Change is inevitable.

In a universe balanced and held together with opposites, change is inevitable.

The discomfort in change isn't because of the change itself: it's our resistance to change that hurts.

Resistance is the sand between the sandpaper and the wood: it tears the wood down.

Remove the sand, the resistance, and its movement is smooth; it's good. Keep the sand, the resistance, and the wood is smoothed; it's good.

It's all change, It's all Good.

## _Day 348_

**It's all Good.**

Joys are simply one side of a two-sided coin, and so is pain.

Without both, there would be no coin. When one comes, the other is close behind.

See them both as Good; part of God' system of laws keeping a balance to the universe. Accept them as part of the greater Good. The more we can see this the more "bad" and "good" will no longer be a matter of circumstance, but instead a choice.

## _Day 349_

**Today's Lesson:**

Keep it simple.

## _Day 350_

**Today's assignment:**

Go stand in front of a mirror. Look yourself in the
eyes. Don't look away. Tell yourself the following:

"I love you."

"I forgive you for what you've done wrong to me and
others."

"Today your limitations are behind you."

"Today you are reborn."

"Today we begin again."

Smile.

## _Day 351_

### Today's assignment:

1.  Pray for others.

2.  Keep positive mental beliefs and positive thoughts of others.

3.  Cheer people up.

4.  Help others to see things in a forgiving and loving light.

5.  Give unneeded material things; old clothes, money, furniture, etc.

6.  Harmonize relations between others.

# *Day 352*

## Today's assignment:

1.  Seek the good in those around you.

2.  Inspire hope.

3.  Promote forgiveness.

4.  Give others the benefit of any doubt, not prejudging which is prejudice.

5.  Pray for the world.

6.  Let others go first.

7.  Smile at people.

8.  Give of your time, a listening ear, your attention, a helping hand.

9.  Do good deeds in secret. Make this a fun challenge.

10. Make random acts of kindness.

You will find these the single most prosperous actions you can take for yourself.

# _Day 353_

**Contemplate study, meditate on, and practice these:**

1. Give and Serve
2. Have Faith
3. Have the ability to release and Let Go
4. Be Honest with self and with others
5. Have an Open Mind
6. Be Trustworthy
7. Show Compassion
8. Practice Kindness
9. Be Just and Fair
10. Have Loyalty
11. Be Flexible and open to change
12. Be Loving
13. Practice Selflessness
14. Be Helpful
15. Be Courteous

## _Day 354_

**Contemplate study, meditate on, and practice these:**

1.  Be Positive in word and action

2.  Be Forgiving

3.  Be Humble

4.  Have Gratitude

5.  Have Appreciation

6.  Express Thankfulness

7.  Practice Self-restraint, Self-control

8.  Listen to your inner voice for guidance

9.  Be Attentive to the present moment

10. Have Understanding

11. Be Accepting

12. Have Balance

13. Be Enthusiastic

14. Be Generous

15. Be Hopeful and be a bringer of Hope

## *Day 355*

**Contemplate study, meditate on, and practice these:**

1. Practice mindfulness

2. Be Patience

3. Have Perseverance

4. Unify

5. Sincerity

6. Be Simple

7. Remain Teachable

8. Seek and see the Divine in all

…and more will be revealed through all of these once experienced at deeper levels. So go and teach. Speak the truth but surely live it to complete your lesson.

## *Day 356*

**Be the positive one.**

Be the one who points out the possibilities.

## _Day 357_

**The positive one**

People are drawn to and attracted to the uplifting,

the enthusiastic and the positive.

Use this power wisely.

If used for selfish purposes, you will fall.

If used for good, you shall prosper.

Choose well.


## _Day 358_

**It's an inside job.**

Once a good habit of thinking is in place it
naturally begins to flow. Remember that it is not by
changing our outside world that we experience our inner
desires, instead as we begin to change the way we see our
world, the world we see changes. So choose well on your
thoughts.

## _Day 359_

**Trust**

Developing Trust is an event of progress, with occasional traces of perfection and demonstration, but always a matter of progress. Practicing and developing Trust is not to be a goal of "getting there," but instead a lifetime moment to moment experience of growth. Our Joy is a byproduct of spiritual growth, not of spiritual "got there."

## _Day 360_

### Continually Surrender.

In the freeing of our minds and emotions we become more productive in our spiritual growth, and from that stem harmonious relationships, a productive life, and satisfaction with all circumstance.

## _Day 361_

### Believe

Believe that something wonderful is in store for you today, because it is.

Watch for it, expect it, and give thanks when it comes.

## _Day 362_

### Cherish

Cherish the small things first, from moment to moment.

## _Day 363_

### Keep Right

Keep right with everyone. As if today was your last in this body, for it very well could be. What would you want to be remembered for, what is left undone?

Always right your wrongs immediately, always say I love you.

Make everyday your last day. In doing this we learn to cherish our time, our influences, our family, our friends, and their memories of us.

# _Day 364_

## Journal

Journal daily: it's a powerful emotional detoxification.

Put it on paper.

A few other uses include: If angry, write a letter to the person, and then throw it away. If troubled, put it on paper and mail it to yourself. When you get it, read it and see how not a big deal it really was.

Use this tool as needed.

## _Day 365_

**Turn**

When tempted to argue, be silent instead.

When tempted to criticize, compliment instead.

When tempted to gossip, walk away instead.

Do the opposite, it will amaze others, and it feels great!

## *The Spiritual Life*

The spiritual life isn't about escaping life, it's about coming more fully into this gift we call life. It's about seeing the gifts, appreciating the small things, cherishing our fellows on this journey, accepting each other's beliefs, demonstrating goodwill, teaching, revealing the Good in the bad, connecting and staying connected, being free, spreading kindness, sharing love, trusting God, seeing the similarities, noticing the coincidences, giving thanks for the alignments, understanding that everything has a purpose, that all things and circumstance can have value, that everything holds a lesson, to experience it all open and freely, connecting with our planet, putting feet on the grass and toes in the sand, hearing the birds and thanking them for their song, feeling the rain and thanking it for its cleansing, being thankful for life yet understanding and accepting that part of life is that it changes, that we change, that we transition. Like the seasons show us, nature and the like, all things are made anew. We are made anew, everyday, again, and again, and again.

Be new, savor each moment, and keep an open heart.

For correspondence with the author email him at
Aw8kning@aol.com

Printed in Great Britain
by Amazon

86203873R00098